PowerKids Readers:

The Bilingual Library of the
United States of America™

MASSACHUSETTS

JOSÉ MARÍA OBREGÓN

TRADUCCIÓN AL ESPAÑOL: MARÍA CRISTINA BRUSCA

The Rosen Publishing Group's
PowerKids Press™ & **Editorial Buenas Letras**™
New York

Published in 2006 by The Rosen Publishing Group, Inc.
29 East 21st Street, New York, NY 10010

First Edition

Book Design: Albert B. Hanner
Photo Credits: Cover © Bill Ross/Corbis; p. 5 Albert B. Hanner; p. 7 © 2002 Geoatlas; pp. 9, 23 © James Marshall/Corbis; pp. 11, 13, 15, 17, 31 (Dickenson, Kennedy, Kerouac, Pilgrims) © Bettmann/Corbis; p. 19 © Royalty-Free/Corbis; p. 21 © Farrell Grehan/Corbis; pp. 25, 30 (Capital) © David Sailors/Corbis; p. 30 (Mayflower) © Hal Horwitz/Corbis; p. 30 (Chickadee) © Arthur Morris/Corbis; pp. 30 (The Bay State), 31 (Marina)© Kevin Fleming/Corbis; p. 30 (American Elm) © Christie's Images/Corbis; p. 31 (Anthony) © Corbis; p. 31 (Geisel) © James L. Amos/Corbis; p. 31 (Bush) © Christopher J. Morris/Corbis

Library of Congress Cataloging-in-Publication Data

Obregón, José María, 1963–
Massachusetts / José María Obregón ; traducción al español, María Cristina Brusca.— 1st ed.
   p. cm. — (The bilingual library of the United States of America) In English and Spanish.
Includes bibliographical references and index.
ISBN 1-4042-3086-6 (lib. bdg.)
1. Massachusetts–Juvenile literature. I. Title. II. Series.
F64.3.O27 2006
974.4–dc22
                                        2005008351

Manufactured in the United States of America

Due to the changing nature of Internet links, Editorial Buenas Letras has developed an online list of Web sites related to the subject of this book. This site is updated regularly. Please use this link to access the list:

http://www.buenasletraslinks.com/ls/massachusetts

Contents

Contenido

Welcome to Massachusetts

These are the flag and seal of the state of Massachusetts. John Hancock, the first governor of Massachusetts, adopted the seal in 1780.

Bienvenidos a Massachusetts

Estos son la bandera y el escudo de Massachusetts. En 1780, John Hanckock, primer gobernador de Massachusetts, adoptó el escudo del estado.

Massachusetts Flag and State Seal

Bandera y escudo de Massachusetts

Massachusetts Geography

Massachusetts borders the states of New Hampshire, Vermont, New York, Connecticut, and Rhode Island. Massachusetts has two large islands. They are Martha's Vineyard and Nantucket.

Geografía de Massachusetts

Massachusetts linda con los estados de Nuevo Hampshire, Vermont, Nueva York, Connecticut y Rhode Island. Massachusetts tiene dos islas grandes, Martha's Vineyard y Nantucket.

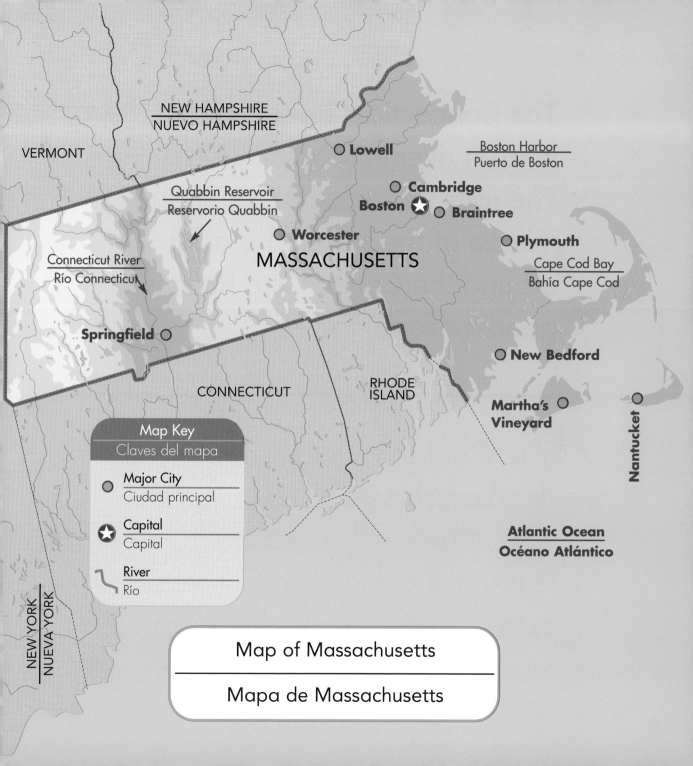

VERMONT

NEW HAMPSHIRE
NUEVO HAMPSHIRE

○ **Lowell**

Boston Harbor
Puerto de Boston

Quabbin Reservoir
Reservorio Quabbin

○ **Cambridge**
Boston ⭐
○ **Braintree**

○ **Worcester**

MASSACHUSETTS

○ **Plymouth**

Cape Cod Bay
Bahía Cape Cod

Connecticut River
Río Connecticut

Springfield ○

CONNECTICUT

RHODE
ISLAND

○ **New Bedford**

Martha's ○
Vineyard

○ Nantucket

Map Key
Claves del mapa

○ **Major City**
Ciudad principal

⭐ **Capital**
Capital

〰 **River**
Río

NEW YORK
NUEVA YORK

Atlantic Ocean
Océano Atlántico

Map of Massachusetts

Mapa de Massachusetts

The Connecticut River is the longest river in Massachusetts. The river runs south through the middle of the state. The area around the Connecticut River is good for farming.

El río Connecticut es el río más largo de Massachusetts. El río corre hacia el sur atravesando el estado. La región que rodea al río Connecticut es muy buena para la agricultura.

The Connecticut River

Río Connecticut

Massachusetts History

Massachusetts is named after the Massachuset Indians. The Massachuset were one of the Native American peoples that lived in the area before the arrival of the European settlers.

Historia de Massachusetts

Massachusetts tomó su nombre de la tribu Massachuset. Los Massachuset eran uno de los pueblos indígenas norteamericanos que vivían en la región antes de la llegada de los colonos europeos.

Massachuset Indians

Indios Massachuset

In 1620, 102 men, women, and children arrived at Plymouth, Massachusetts. They had sailed from England on the *Mayflower*. They are known as the Pilgrims. The Pilgrims founded one of the first European colonies in North America.

En 1620, 102 hombres, mujeres y niños llegaron a Plymouth, Massachusetts. Habían navegado desde Inglaterra en el Mayflower. Se les conoce como los Peregrinos. Los Peregrinos fundaron una de las primeras colonias europeas de América del Norte.

The Landing of the Pilgrims at Plymouth

Llegada de los Peregrinos a Plymouth

John Adams was born in Braintree, Massachusetts, in 1735. He was a leader of the group that claimed independence from Great Britain. He became the second president of the United States in 1797.

John Adams nació en Braintree, Massachusetts, en 1735. Adams fue un líder del grupo que reclamó la independencia de Gran Bretaña. En 1797, llegó a ser el segundo presidente de los Estados Unidos.

John Adams

Phillis Wheatley was born in Africa and was brought to Massachusetts as a slave in 1761. When she was 13 she began to write poetry. In 1773, she became the first African American poet to publish a book.

Phillis Wheatley nació en África y fue traída a Massachusetts, como esclava, en 1761. Cuando tenía 13 años comenzó a escribir poesía. En 1773, Wheatley publicó un libro de poemas. Wheatley fue la primera persona de raza negra en publicar un libro.

In 1773, Phillis Wheatley Gained Her Freedom

En 1773, Phillis Wheatley recuperó su libertad

Living in Massachusetts

Boston is the largest city in Massachusetts and the capital of the state. It is also one of the oldest cities in the United States.

La vida en Massachusetts

Boston es la ciudad más grande de Massachusetts y la capital del estado. Es también una de las ciudades más antiguas de los Estados Unidos.

Boston and the Charles River

Boston y el río Charles

Massachusetts has some of the best universities in the country. Students from all over the world come to study at these schools. Harvard University and the Massachusetts Institute of Technology (MIT) are in the city of Cambridge.

Massachusetts tiene algunas de las mejores universidades del país. Estudiantes de todo el mundo vienen a estudiar a estas escuelas. La Universidad de Harvard y el Instituto Tecnológico de Massachusetts (MIT) están en la ciudad de Cambridge.

Harvard University

Universidad de Harvard

Cape Cod Bay is a favorite spot for the people of Massachusetts and its visitors. A bay is an area of sea surrounded by some land. People enjoy the ocean views and the marinas along the bay.

La bahía Cape Cod es el lugar favorito de la gente de Massachusetts y de sus visitantes. Una bahía es un área de mar rodeada, en parte, de tierra. La gente disfruta de los paisajes marítimos y de los puertos que hay a lo largo de la bahía.

The Provincetown Marina in Cape Cod

Puerto Provincetown en Cape Cod

Boston, Worcester, Springfield, Lowell, and Cambridge are important cities in Massachusetts. The goverment of the state works in the Massachusetts State House in Boston.

Boston, Worcester, Springfield, Lowell y Cambridge son ciudades importantes de Massachusetts. La administración del gobierno del estado trabaja en la Casa de Gobierno de Massachusetts, en Boston.

Massachusetts State House in Boston

Casa de Gobierno de Massachusetts

Activity:
Let´s Draw the Map of Massachusetts

Actividad:
Dibujemos el mapa de Massachusetts

1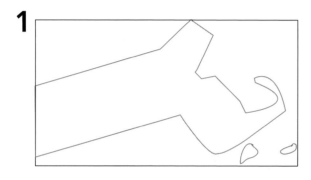

Draw a rectangle. Next draw a rough guide of the shape of the state.

Dibuja un rectángulo. Luego traza un esquema de la forma del estado.

2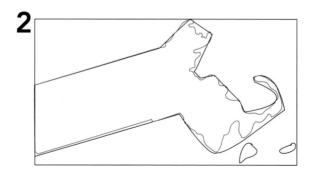

Inside the rough guide draw the outline of the state.

Dentro del esquema dibuja los bordes del estado.

3

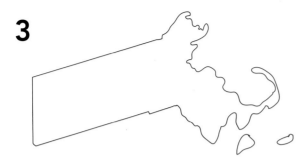

Erase the extra lines. You may need to redraw some edges.

Borra las líneas innecesarias. Quizás tengas que retocar el dibujo de los bordes.

To finish, shade the state.
a) Draw a five-pointed star for Boston.
b) Draw a wavy line for the Connecticut River.
c) Use a circle to mark Plymouth.
d) Draw a triangle for Harvard University.

4

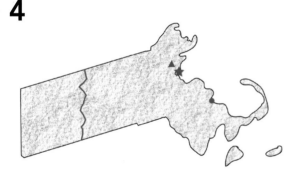

Para terminar, sombrea el estado.
a) Dibuja una estrella de cinco puntas en el lugar de Boston.
b) Traza una línea ondulada para indicar el río Connecticut.
c) Marca Plymouth con un círculo.
d) Marca con un triángulo el sitio de la Universidad de Harvard.

Timeline		Cronología
The Pilgrims arrive in Plymouth and set up a colony.	1620	Los Peregrinos llegan a Plymouth y fundan una colonia.
Pilgrims celebrate the first Thanksgiving.	1621	Los Peregrinos celebran el primer Día de Acción de Gracias.
The Boston Tea Party takes place.	1773	Se produce la Fiesta del Té de Boston.
The first subway system in the United States opens in Boston.	1898	Se inaugura en Boston el primer sistema de trenes subterráneos de los Estados Unidos.
The Massachusetts Institute of Technology (MIT) develops the first computer.	1928	El Instituto Tecnológico de Massachusetts (MIT) desarrolla la primera computadora.
Massachusetts senator John F. Kennedy is elected president of the United States.	1960	Un senador de Massachusetts, John F. Kennedy, es elegido presidente de los Estados Unidos.
Jane Swift becomes the first woman to serve as governor of Massachusetts.	2001	Jane Swift es la primera mujer en servir como gobernadora de Massachusetts.

Massachusetts Events

Eventos en Massachusetts

April
Boston Marathon

Abril
Maratón de Boston

May
Figawi Sailboat Race in Cape Cod

Mayo
Regata Figawi, en Cape Cod

June
Jacob's Pillow Dance Festival

Junio
Festival de danza Jacob's Pillow

July
Barnstable County Fair
in East Falmouth

Julio
Feria del Condado de Barnstable,
en East Falmouth

September
Taste of Boston
Brimfield Antique Show
The Big E in West Springfield.

Septiembre
El sabor de Boston
Exposición de antigüedades de Brimfield
The Big E, en West Springfield

October
Nantucket Arts Festival
Northeast Sea Glass Festival
in Rockport
Topsfield Fair, America's Oldest
Agricultural Fair
Haunted Happenings in Salem

Octubre
Festival de las Artes de Nantucket
Festival noreste del vidrio de mar,
en Rockport
Feria Topsfield, la feria agrícola
más antigüa de América
Espectáculos encantados, en Salem

December
Christmas Stroll in Nantucket

Diciembre
Posadas de Navidad, en Nantucket

Massachusetts Facts/Datos sobre Massachusets

Population
6.3 million

Población
6.3 millones

Capital
Boston

Capital
Boston

State Motto
By the sword we seek peace,
but peace only under liberty

Lema del estado
Con nuestra espada
buscamos la paz, pero
la paz solo en libertad

State Flower
Mayflower

Flor del estado
Flor de mayo

State Bird
Chickadee

Ave del estado
Carbonero de
capucha negra

State Nickname
The Bay State

Mote del estado
Estado de la Bahía

State Tree
American Elm

Árbol del estado
Olmo americano

State Song
"All Hail to Massachusetts"

Canción del estado
"Saludamos a
Massachusetts"

Famous Massachusitens/
Massachusetanos famosos

Susan B. Anthony
(1820–1906)

Activist
Activista

Emily Dickinson
(1830–1886)

Poet
Poeta

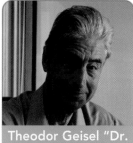

Theodor Geisel "Dr. Seuss" *(1904–1991)*

Children's author
Autor de libros infantiles

John F. Kennedy
(1917–1963)

U.S. president
Presidente de E.U.A.

Jack Kerouac
(1922–1969)

Author
Escritor

George H. W. Bush
(1924–   )

U.S. president
Presidente de E.U.A.

Words to Know/Palabras que debes saber

bay
bahía

border
frontera

pilgrims
peregrinos

marina
puerto

Here are more books to read about Massachusetts:
Otros libros que puedes leer sobre Massachusets:

In English/En inglés:

Massachusetts
Rookie Read-About Geography
by De Capua, Sarah
Children's Press, 2003

Massachusetts
Hello USA
by J. F. Warner
Lerner Publications, 2001

Words in English: 335

Palabras en español: 348

Index

Índice